Original title:
Misty Creases Within the Griffin Wool

Author: Aron Pilviste
ISBN HARDBACK: 978-1-80563-021-0
ISBN PAPERBACK: 978-1-80564-542-9

The Allure of Forgotten Whispers

In the heart of the forest, where shadows play,
Old oaks stand guard, holding secrets at bay.
Whispers like breezes drift soft through the leaves,
Memories linger, like dust on the eaves.

Ghostly echoes of laughter, from ages long past,
Dance in the twilight, though fading so fast.
With each murmured promise the night softly sighs,
Under the blanket of star-laden skies.

The stones tell their stories, with moss-covered grace,
Of heroes and lovers who once found their place.
Hidden in shadows, enchantments still glow,
Painted in twilight, where moonlight serves low.

Ancient paths beckon, with footfalls of fate,
Leading seekers onward, though darkness may wait.
Each step is a stitch in a tapestry grand,
Woven with threads of both time and the land.

So listen, dear wanderer, heed the soft calls,
For the forest remembers, through rise and through falls.
In whispers forgotten, new dreams may ignite,
As you wander the realm between shadow and light.

Veils of Sweet Enchantment

In shadows where the moonlight glows,
Whispers of magic in the rose,
A soft breeze carries secrets spun,
As playful spirits dance and run.

With dreams entwined in silken threads,
Through ancient woods where silence spreads,
The night is filled with sparkling light,
A tapestry woven, pure delight.

Each glance reveals a hidden fate,
Where wishes linger, love awaits,
A world awash in twilight's gleam,
Enticing hearts, enchanting dream.

Beneath the stars, where stories weave,
The heart of night, a sweet reprieve,
In every breath, adventure calls,
A symphony of magic falls.

In veils of gold, the dawn ascends,
A promise whispered as night ends,
Yet still within that fading night,
The echoes of enchantment light.

Threads of Silence in the Night

When twilight's cloak begins to fall,
The world awaits a hushed enthrall,
In slumber's grasp, the shadows creep,
Awakening dreams from gentle sleep.

A silver thread, a whispered sigh,
Carried far beneath the sky,
In quietude where moments freeze,
Night weaves its song among the trees.

The stars align in patterns rare,
Each twinkle holds a secret stare,
A lullaby soft as a feather,
Threads of silence bind us together.

In hidden glades where lanterns glow,
Mysteries of the night unfold,
And with each hush, a tale ignites,
In fabric stitched by silver lights.

The night may fade with burning morn,
Yet in its heart, we're never worn,
For in the dark, sweet dreams take flight,
In threads of silence, pure and bright.

A Tapestry of Lore Beneath the Stars

In starlit skies where wishes soar,
Each glimmer tells of tales of yore,
A tapestry of lore unfolds,
As ancient as the stars it holds.

The echoes of a time gone by,
In whispered winds that softly sigh,
The moon hangs low, a listening ear,
To every secret we revere.

Beneath the heavens' canvas vast,
The present meets the distant past,
We gather dreams like fallen leaves,
In stories spun, our heart believes.

Through constellations, tales entwine,
Each story weaves a thread divine,
And in the quiet, magic stirs,
In the night's embrace, our spirit purrs.

So when the stars begin to gleam,
Recall the beauty of the dream,
For in their light, the world is free,
A tapestry for you and me.

Whirlwinds of Dreams in Soft Haze

Amidst the mist where shadows play,
Whirlwinds of dreams softly sway,
In gentle tides, the heart explores,
As night unveils its secret stores.

Embers dance beneath pale light,
Casting spells upon the night,
And in the fragile air we breathe,
A thousand hopes begin to weave.

Each breath a promise in disguise,
As starlit visions gain their rise,
The world spins on in soft embrace,
Carried by time's unyielding grace.

Like fleeting whispers on the breeze,
The heart finds solace, hope, and ease,
In every corner, dreams ignite,
In swirling mists, we chase the light.

So let your spirit take its flight,
Through whirlwinds of enchanted night,
For in the soft haze, you'll find peace,
In dreams where endless joys increase.

Echoes of the Enchanted Realm

In twilight's glow, the magic sighs,
With whispers soft as starlit skies.
Creatures stir in hidden glades,
Their laughter woven through the shades.

Beneath the boughs of ancient trees,
A tale unfolds upon the breeze.
Mysteries wrapped in silver mist,
Where shadows dance, and dreams persist.

The brook sings songs of ages past,
Each note a spell, each ripple cast.
In every stone, a secret lies,
A world reborn as daylight dies.

Echoes linger, hearts entwined,
In realms where time itself is blind.
With every step, a journey starts,
As starlight kisses waiting hearts.

So venture forth, let wonder bloom,
Within this land, dispel the gloom.
Embrace the magic, let it stay,
For in this realm, you're free to play.

Whispers of the Forest's Heart

Amidst the trees, the secrets hum,
Each leaf a note, a gentle drum.
The path ahead, a winding thread,
That leads to dreams where spirits tread.

Sunbeams weave through emerald lace,
In this enchanted, sacred space.
The forest breathes, its spirit strong,
A symphony, an ancient song.

Mossy carpets beneath our feet,
In every corner, tales replete.
From silver streams to soaring heights,
The heart of nature ignites the nights.

Whispers float on fragrant air,
Calling forth both brave and rare.
In shadowed glens where magic thrives,
The forest holds our truth alive.

So listen close when silence falls,
The ancient wisdom gently calls.
In every rustle, in every bark,
The whispers lead us through the dark.

Fabric of Dreams in Ethereal Light

In twilight's loom, the dreams are spun,
With threads of hope, the day is done.
Each stitch a wish, each knot a sigh,
A tapestry against the sky.

Ethereal light, so soft and warm,
Weaves a promise, a gentle balm.
In cosmic dance, the stars align,
Creating patterns, both grand and fine.

Through this fabric, stories flow,
Of whispered love and gentle woe.
A glimmer here, a shadow there,
In this realm, our hearts laid bare.

With every thread, our souls unite,
In dreams that shimmer, pure and bright.
Together we stitch hopes and fears,
In the fabric spun from all our years.

So reach for stars with hands outstretched,
In woven dreams, our hearts enmeshed.
For in this light, we find our place,
A dance of shadows, a warm embrace.

Breaths of Fog Wrapped in Sweetness

In morning fog, the world awakes,
With soft embrace that gently shakes.
The air is sweet, like honeyed dreams,
Where time dissolves in silver streams.

Each breath we take, a whispered tune,
As dawn unfolds beneath the moon.
The hills are clad in misty veils,
Where nature spins her tender tales.

With every step, the quiet swells,
As nature's secret magic dwells.
In woodland paths and meadows bright,
The soul finds peace in morning light.

Wrapped in fog, our worries fade,
As laughter breaks the solemn shade.
With every heart, we share this bliss,
A bond created in tender kiss.

So let us breathe this sweetness in,
With every moment, let love begin.
In fog's embrace, we find our peace,
As life's symphony finds its release.

Whispers of Warmth Beneath the Shroud

In the quiet, shadows creep,
Softly where the secrets sleep.
Haunted by the stars' faint glow,
Whispers dance where breezes flow.

Beneath the veil of silver night,
Dreams awaken, take to flight.
Fingertips of twilight grace,
Cradle hearts in soft embrace.

Beneath the shroud of tender mist,
Echoes of a fleeting tryst.
Gentle laughter, soft as air,
Calls to those who wander there.

In the hush, a warmth is found,
Lingering where hopes abound.
In a world where shadows blend,
Whispers promise, never end.

So close your eyes, let magic stir,
The warmth awakens, you can purr.
Find the light within your soul,
Let the whispers make you whole.

Secrets of the Fabled Winds

Across the hills, the soft winds sigh,
Carrying tales from long gone by.
Secrets swirl in each gentle breeze,
Holding mysteries beneath the trees.

Listen closely, hear their call,
Stories echo, rise and fall.
Winds that wander, wild and free,
Kiss the edges of the sea.

In every gust, a legend spun,
Of kingdoms lost, and battles won.
Fabled dreams the winds bestow,
Whispered tales of what we know.

As shadows weave through evening's light,
Dance with echoes of the night.
Every breeze a fleeting ghost,
Haunting hearts that need it most.

So let the winds guide you near,
Embrace the whispers you can hear.
Sumptuous secrets, tender, bold,
In fabled winds, their stories told.

Threads Kissing the Misty Aether

In the realm where dreams entwine,
Threads of fate in silence shine.
Misty echoes kiss the air,
Woven whispers, rich and rare.

A tapestry of starlit gleams,
Comes alive within our dreams.
Each strand sings a lullaby,
Soft as leaves that float and fly.

Through the mist, a figure glides,
On the path where magic bides.
Every step a secret shared,
In the aether, none compared.

As twilight fades to silken night,
Threads shimmer in the softest light.
Feel the pull, the gentle tug,
Of fate's embrace, a tender hug.

So walk the line between the worlds,
As starlit dreams unfurl and swirled.
In the mist, our stories weave,
In whispered threads, we shall believe.

The Guardian's Sigh in the Dusk

As day surrenders to the night,
A guardian whispers, bathed in light.
With each sigh, a promise made,
In the dusk, where dreams cascade.

Watch the stars ignite the skies,
As shadows dance, and magic flies.
Tender moments, fragile, sweet,
The guardian's heart skips a beat.

In the twilight's gentle embrace,
A fleeting chill, a soft trace.
Lost secrets vanish in the glow,
Inviting hearts to dream and flow.

Whispers linger on the air,
Held by those who truly care.
Beneath the watchful, silent gaze,
We find our peace in the dusk's haze.

So rest your head and close your eyes,
Let the guardian's soft sighs,
Carry you to realms anew,
Where magic lives and dreams come true.

Where Sorcery Meets Silken Strands

In twilight's grasp, the spell is cast,
With silken threads that weave so fast.
A whispered charm, a flickering light,
Binding the shadows to the night.

The weavers dance in moonlit glow,
Crafting secrets for the brave to know.
Each stitch a tale of magic spun,
Where all the worlds converge as one.

Through silken strands, the visions flow,
A tapestry of dreams to show.
In every knot, a fate entwined,
With every twist, a heart aligned.

As sorcery and silk embrace,
The mysteries unfold with grace.
In the quiet, magic stirs,
A realm where wonder softly purrs.

So journey forth, dear wanderer bold,
In silk and sorcery, tales unfold.
For treasures lie in threads of fate,
Where magic whispers, never late.

Veils of Fog on Feathered Dreams

Amidst the fog that shrouds the morn,
Feathers fall, the night's forlorn.
With every flutter, secrets sigh,
As dreams take flight in whispered sky.

The veils weave tales like gossamer lace,
Embracing all in their soft embrace.
Through misty realms where shadows play,
The heart's desires find their way.

In silver light, the feathers gleam,
Caught in the threads of a haunting dream.
A waltz of fog, a shadowed grace,
Where fears and hopes oft interlace.

Each feather holds a wish untold,
Of courage fierce and hearts so bold.
In twilight's mist, the dreams shall soar,
Until the dawn opens wide its door.

So dance within this hushed delight,
Where fog and feathers blur the night.
For every veil, a story spun,
In whispered dreams, all hearts are won.

Whispering Shadows of the Enchanted

In corners dark where shadows creep,
Whispers echo, secrets deep.
The enchanted woods hold tales of old,
In whispered tones, their magic told.

Beneath the boughs, where fairies dwell,
Each shadow speaks of lore to tell.
In twilight's glow, the mysteries weave,
Entrancing spells for those who believe.

With every rustle, a voice divine,
Inviting wanderers to entwine.
In dreams both wild and dreams so pure,
The shadows beckon, hearts allure.

As stars align in cosmic dance,
The whispered call of fate's romance.
Through veils of night, the magic flows,
In every shadow, enchantment grows.

So tread with care in twilight's realm,
Where shadows whisper, magic's helm.
For those who listen, secrets gleam,
In the enchanted night's eternal dream.

Secrets Woven in Ethereal Threads

In twilight's loom, the threads are spun,
Ethereal secrets, never done.
A tapestry of dreams unfolds,
With every stitch, a story told.

The weavers' hands, they gently move,
Crafting patterns, hearts to prove.
In whispers soft like morning dew,
The threads reveal what's brave and true.

Through silken cords, the tales unite,
Binding hopes beneath starlit night.
Each twist and turn, a secret clasp,
In every weave, a wish to grasp.

As shadows dance with gentle grace,
The ethereal threads find their place.
In the fabric of the night sky vast,
The future whispers of the past.

So linger long in the twilight glow,
Where woven secrets softly flow.
For in the threads, the magic lies,
In every heart, a dream will rise.

A Tapestry of Hidden Beasts

In the thicket, shadows play,
Secret creatures weave away.
Whispers of fur and echoing calls,
Nature's canvas silently sprawls.

Moonlit glades where spirits roam,
Each hidden beast calls this place home.
Gentle paws on leafy ground,
In stillness, their magic is found.

Eyes like lanterns, gleaming bright,
Guiding dreamers through the night.
A tapestry woven with care,
Each thread a story, rich and rare.

Softly they dance, in twilight's grace,
Mysterious beings, no need to chase.
For those who seek, the world bestows,
A glimpse of life that softly glows.

In tangled woods where fears will cease,
Every heartbeat whispers peace.
For amidst the dark, a truth reveals,
The hidden beasts, their magic feels.

Celestial Hues in Fleecy Whispers

In clouds adorned with silver lace,
Colors dance in a soft embrace.
Celestial hues of twilight's sigh,
As stars awaken in the sky.

Each fleecy whisper carries dreams,
Drifting softly like silver streams.
Fleeting moments on the breeze,
Nature's palette, meant to please.

With each twilight, the heavens glow,
Painting tales of long ago.
A tapestry of night unfurls,
As thoughts take flight in endless swirls.

In the stillness, secrets swirl,
Echoes of a starlit world.
Every twinkle, a promise made,
Wrapped in dreams that never fade.

So look above and find your place,
In every hue, a trace of grace.
For in celestial realms we find,
A flurry of magic, wild and kind.

Chasing Shadows in an Ancient Grove

In ancient groves where whispers dwell,
Secrets of the past cast a spell.
Leaves above, a rustling choir,
Echoing tales of forgotten fire.

Chasing shadows, we wander deep,
Where ancient trees their vigils keep.
With gnarled roots and mossy tears,
Every step unveils lost years.

Time drips slow like honey's grace,
Each lingering moment finds its place.
In the heart of the grove, we roam,
In every shadow, a sense of home.

Beneath the boughs, old spirits sigh,
In whispers woven, they float nigh.
Through tangled paths and hidden bends,
The mysteries of time, our hearts attend.

So heed the call of fragrant air,
Let the ancient spirits share.
For in their guidance, we will see,
The beauty of our history.

Enigmatic Serendipity in Night's Cloak

Beneath the night's enchanting veil,
Serendipity spins a tale.
Stars align in cryptic grace,
Whispers linger in moonlit space.

In every shadow, chance appears,
An unexpected thrill that cheers.
Moments collide like silk and stone,
In the quiet dark, we're not alone.

Velvet skies hold secrets near,
As dreams waltz in, casting fear.
In the stillness, magic brews,
Inviting hearts to chase their hues.

Follow the path where silence gleams,
And let the night weave tangled dreams.
For serendipity, sweetly spun,
Awaits each heart, a gift undone.

So as the stars twinkle their song,
Embrace the night and wander long.
For every twist, a chance to find,
The enigmatic threads that bind.

Enigma Wrapped in a Furry Embrace

In a grove where whispers dwell,
A creature stirs with secrets to tell,
Fur like dusk, eyes aflame,
It beckons softly, calling your name.

Moonlight dances on leaves so fair,
A magic lingers, thick in the air,
With every pawstep, shadows spin,
A glance reveals where dreams begin.

Through tangled vines and twilight mist,
The enigmatic allure, hard to resist,
Silhouetted against starlit skies,
Entwined in tales, where wonder lies.

Step closer now, don't shy away,
Let the furry whisper lead your way,
For in its gaze, the world expands,
A doorway waits in unseen lands.

With a rustle, the spirit fades,
Yet left behind, the magic invades,
In your heart, forever lace,
The enigma clothed in furry embrace.

Breath of the Chimeric Dawn

On the horizon, colors weave,
A tapestry the morn shall cleave,
With wings of wonder, dreams take flight,
A jeweled sunrise banishes night.

Chimeras rise in vibrant hues,
With whispers of forgotten clues,
They dance in grace, a fleeting sight,
Painting dawn with pure delight.

Beneath the glow, the shadows play,
In realms where night has lost its sway,
Each breath is laced with magic's thrill,
As day awakens, hearts do fill.

Ethereal notes, a symphony,
Call forth the day's sweet melody,
In every heart, a quiet song,
Together we join, where dreams belong.

With every step, let laughter chase,
As golden beams paint every face,
In a world reborn, let souls resound,
In the breath of the chimeric dawn.

Lurking Shadows of the Faery Realm

In the twilight where secrets bloom,
Shadows stir, dispelling gloom,
Flickering lights in emerald glade,
A faery dance in whispers played.

Among the trees, the laughter twirls,
As night unfolds its silken curls,
With every flicker, a story spins,
Of ancient tales where magic begins.

With nimble footsteps and glistening eyes,
They flit like dreams, beneath starlit skies,
Guardians of whimsy, elusive yet near,
Hypnotic songs for those who hear.

Darkness deepens, but hope remains,
For in their laughter, freedom gains,
With every heartbeat, shadows blend,
In the faery realm, where magic transcends.

So heed the call when dusk descends,
For in such places, time bends,
Embrace the mystery that gently hums,
Lurking shadows, where wonder comes.

The Allure of Fog-Cloaked Whimsy

In a world wrapped in silvery shroud,
Whimsy whispers, soft yet loud,
Through rolling fog, a tale unfurls,
Imagination spins in swirling swirls.

Wanderers roam in mystery's embrace,
With each step, they're lost in grace,
The air is thick with dreams untold,
As the fog weaves stories bold.

Creatures of light, in shadows they bask,
With twinkling laughter, their only task,
To lure the weary, invite them near,
As magic drips from murmurings clear.

Delightful echoes dwell in the mist,
A treasure trove of dreams to assist,
Through every twist, curiosity grows,
In the fog-cloaked pathways, enchantment flows.

So follow the whispers, heed the call,
For in the fog, there's beauty for all,
The allure of whimsy, soft and profound,
In the shrouded wonder, let joy abound.

Shadows Play Amongst Celestial Threads

In twilight's embrace, shadows weave,
A tapestry where dreams believe.
Celestial threads on the starlit ground,
Whispering secrets, soft and profound.

A dance of light, where echoes reside,
Under the moon, where hopes coincide.
The nightingale sings to the dreams that depart,
Painting the darkness, a work of art.

With mysteries wrapped in velvet night,
Stars twinkle softly, a beacon of light.
The cosmos hums a harmonious song,
Drawing the weary where they belong.

Amidst the stars, the shadows play,
Guiding the lost on their winding way.
Through silver skies, they gently sway,
In the realm of dreams where wishes stay.

So linger awhile in this sacred space,
Where shadows and stars find their embrace.
For in this realm, our spirits soar,
As shadows dance forevermore.

Guardians of the Whispering Mists

In realms where whispers weave and twine,
Guardians watch with eyes divine.
Through veils of fog, they roam the night,
Guarding secrets out of sight.

Each misty breath tells tales untold,
Of ancient magic and hearts of gold.
Beneath the silvered, moonlit glow,
Their silent vigil, steady and slow.

With every pulse, the shadows stir,
In the quiet depths, their spirits blur.
They cradle dreams and fears alike,
Showing paths where souls might hike.

Among the trees, their presence sways,
In nature's heart, where enchantment plays.
The mist wraps round like a gentle sigh,
A guardian's promise woven high.

So heed the whispers in the night,
For every shadow holds a light.
Within the mists, a truth we find,
That all are guardians, intertwined.

The Enigma of Hidden Feathers

Beneath the veil of twilight's grace,
Lie secrets tucked in a soft embrace.
Feathers whisper tales from above,
Of ancient skies and lost love.

In shadows low, they softly gleam,
Hints of magic in each thin seam.
Mysteries linger where they fall,
Stories waiting for a call.

As time unfolds, the feathers sway,
Carrying wishes that drift away.
In twilight's arms, they take their flight,
Floating softly into the night.

Yet hidden truths within them bide,
Wrapped in silence, they softly hide.
To uncover the stories, we must dare,
To search for feathers scattered in air.

So seek the lost, the soft and small,
In nature's weave, they guide us all.
For every feather holds a tale,
Of dreams remembered, we will sail.

A Symphony in a Celestial Fabric

In the loom of the night, a symphony plays,
Threads of starlight in wondrous arrays.
Each note, a whisper of cosmic delight,
Woven together, shining so bright.

The melodies swirl in the vast expanse,
Drawing the gaze, an enchanting dance.
With every heartbeat, a rhythm unfolds,
A tapestry rich with stories untold.

As comets streak with their fiery embrace,
They join in the music, a heavenly chase.
The universe sings in harmonious tone,
A symphony cherished, never alone.

Echoes of longing weave through the air,
Wrapping the world in their tender care.
In celestial fabric, our dreams take flight,
Guided by starlight through the night.

So let us listen to the cosmic choir,
As constellations weave our heart's desire.
For in this symphony, we find our place,
In the celestial fabric, a warm embrace.

Secrets Bound in Celestial Fluff

In twilight's grasp where whispers dwell,
The stars hold tales too grand to tell.
Beneath the sky, in velvet night,
A tapestry of dreams takes flight.

Clouds drift softly, secrets weave,
In cosmic cradles, hearts believe.
Each shimmer holds a hidden sign,
A world beyond, where hopes align.

The moonlight spills like silver thread,
A gentle balm for fears we dread.
In shadows cast by starlit glow,
The magic of the night will show.

Whispers dance on zephyr's sigh,
As ancient wonders pass us by.
With every pulse of night's embrace,
We find ourselves in time and space.

So gleam, dear stars, with tender care,
For in your light, we're free to dare.
In secrets shared with cosmic trust,
We learn to rise from earthly dust.

Dreams Woven in Gossamer Veils

Through silken paths of twilight shade,
We chase the dreams that time has made.
In every thread, a story spun,
A dance of shadows, night begun.

Gossamer whispers, soft and clear,
Tell tales of hope, of love, of fear.
Each fabric glimmers under the moon,
A symphony of night's sweet tune.

In crafted whims, our wishes grow,
Along the stream where starlights flow.
With every sigh, we weave our fate,
In fragile waltz, we choose our state.

The air is thick with wishes made,
In velvet dreams, we shan't evade.
From depths of night, we seek and find,
The heart's true call, its voice entwined.

Awake, dear souls, to mystery's song,
In realms of night, where we belong.
For every dream, a spark ignites,
In gossamer veils, we chase the lights.

The Murmurs of Ethereal Fleece

In fields of clouds where silence reigns,
The whispers rise like gentle rains.
Each flutter echoes through the night,
A secret song, a soft delight.

Ethereal fleece wraps dreams in peace,
A warm embrace that will not cease.
In every stitch, a hope is sewn,
In twilight's hush, we find our own.

The stars conspire, they flicker bright,
Guiding hearts through the endless night.
Their murmurs swirl like misty air,
In lonesome skies, they softly care.

As moonbeams dance on dewy grass,
We ponder time, as moments pass.
Each twinkling light a fleeting thought,
Of all the dreams we dearly sought.

So let us listen, hearts in tune,
To secrets sung by starlit moon.
In whispers soft, our souls shall glide,
On waves of night, forever ride.

Tangles of Moonlight and Down

In silver strands of moonlit glow,
We find the paths we long to know.
With every twist of gentle night,
We weave the dreams that take to flight.

A tapestry of shadows drawn,
In whispers soft, a brand new dawn.
From spun-out threads of dreamer's lace,
We find our way in time and space.

With each new spark, the night unfolds,
The stories held in silken folds.
In every shimmer, hope is found,
In tangles soft of moonlight's round.

Let downy clouds embrace your heart,
In soft caress, we'll never part.
For in the night's enchanted glow,
The magic weaves, our spirits flow.

So tread lightly on this mystic weave,
Embrace the dreams that you believe.
In tangled light, our fates align,
In moonlit paths, our souls entwine.

The Dance of Veiled Beasts

In moonlit glades where shadows play,
Veiled beasts twirl in a secret ballet.
With eyes that gleam like the stars above,
They dance in silence, a rhythm of love.

Their fur, a cloak of the night's embrace,
Footsteps whisper in time, a gentle pace.
Each paw a story, untold and deep,
In the heart of the forest, where secrets sleep.

Beneath the boughs where the wildflowers bloom,
They weave their tales in the night's soft gloom.
A fleeting glimpse, a magic chance,
Lost in the beauty of their wild dance.

With every twirl, a spell is spun,
In the cool night air, where dreams are won.
The dance goes on, a shimmering sight,
Veiled beasts moving until the first light.

Thus, they vanish at dawn's first glow,
Leaving only whispers of all they know.
In the silence, echoes of their grace,
Stay in the heart, in this hallowed place.

Enchanted Fabrics of the Dawn

As sunlight weaves through leaves in gold,
Fabrics of dawn in colors bold.
Threads of shimmer, stitched with care,
Glisten softly in the morning air.

Each fabric tells of a story spun,
Of dreams awakened, of hope begun.
In violets and blues, the patterns sway,
Whispering secrets of the breaking day.

Starlit memories fade in the light,
Yet in the threads, they hold on tight.
With every fold, a spell is cast,
In the tapestry of moments that fly so fast.

Through the loom of life, we stitch our fate,
In enchanted garments, we create.
When dawn arrives with a gentle hue,
We stand adorned in the dreams we knew.

As the day unfolds in a radiant dance,
We wear our stories, each twist and chance.
With hearts aglow and spirits free,
In enchanted fabrics, we find our glee.

Hushed Whispers in Misty Groves

In the gentle hush of the misty groves,
Whispers of magic in the twilight roves.
Leaves converse with the breeze so light,
Secrets exchanged in the fading night.

The trees lean closer, their branches sway,
Listening keenly to what they may say.
Ghostly murmurs in the cool, damp air,
Stories of ages, beyond compare.

A flicker of light, a sprite takes flight,
Guiding lost souls through the quiet night.
Each whisper carries a tale to unfold,
In the heart of the grove, where legends are told.

Amidst the shadows, in silence profound,
Every rustle of leaves, the softest sound.
In this sacred space where echoes dwell,
Hushed whispers beckon with their spell.

So linger a while, let your heart embrace,
The magic that dances in this hidden place.
In the misty groves, where nature weaves,
Find solace and wonder among the leaves.

Intrigue in a Dream-Spun Tapestry

In a tapestry woven with threads of dreams,
Intrigue unfolds in soft, silken seams.
Each stitch a whisper, each knot a tale,
In a world where shadows and light set sail.

Figures in motion, they twist and gleam,
Visions of futures that shimmer and beam.
What secrets lie in the colorful weave?
A dance of deception, a trick to believe.

As laughter echoes, a mask slips away,
Revealing the truths that in darkness stay.
The colors blend in an enchanting swirl,
A mystery wrapped in a magical curl.

With every glance, the stories entwine,
Life's fragile moments in fabric align.
A fate unwritten, a destiny sown,
In this dream-spun tapestry, we are not alone.

So gaze upon wonders that tease and beguile,
And lose yourself in the dreamer's smile.
For in this creation of art and design,
Lies the beauty of life, forever enshrined.

Twilight's Embrace in a Gilded Shroud

As dusk drapes gold on the weary night,
Whispers of the day take graceful flight.
Stars awaken in the velvet sky,
Dreams unspool as the shadows sigh.

The moon, a sentinel on high,
Watches over with a silvery eye.
With every heartbeat, the world holds fast,
To secrets of future and echoes of past.

Branches dance with a gentle gale,
Tales of enchantment in every trail.
In twilight's grasp, all is set free,
Lost in the magic of what can be.

Beneath the boughs of ancient trees,
Lies the pulse of the evening breeze.
Laughter lingers on soft-spoken lips,
In a realm where reality slips.

So embrace the night with open arms,
For in its haven lie countless charms.
In gilded shrouds, let dreams take flight,
As twilight weaves the tapestry of night.

The Song of the Whispering Woods

Deep within where shadows play,
The woods sing softly at close of day.
Leaves murmur secrets, old and wise,
Guiding the hearts that dare to rise.

A brook hums tunes in tranquil flow,
Winding its way through paths aglow.
Every glen cradles its own refrain,
Notes that linger like a sweetened stain.

Beneath the boughs where elves may tread,
Each whisper echoes where few have led.
Nature holds a concert, soft and clear,
A melody woven for those who hear.

With every footfall, magic stirs,
In the notebook of the mind, it blurs.
Stories play among the ferns and moss,
In the woods where shadows never cross.

So listen close, dear wandering soul,
For in the whispers, you'll find your goal.
The song of the woods is a timeless thread,
Binding the living and the long since dead.

Realm of Fable Enveloped in Mist

In a realm where the fables dwell,
Mysteries weave their own sweet spell.
Veils of mist shroud the hidden land,
Holding tales spun by a gentle hand.

The whispers drift like a feathery sigh,
Glimmers of truth that float and fly.
Distant echoes of laughter ring,
In the hearts of all who dream and sing.

Each step reveals a world anew,
Where wonders wait, fresh as the dew.
Creatures dance in a twilight glow,
Ghosts of legends from long ago.

With every corner, a story unfolds,
In whispers of heroes and treasures untold.
The air is thick with ancient lore,
Inviting the bold to linger and explore.

So wander through this enchanted haze,
Where time is lost in a mystical daze.
For in this realm, the fables insist,
That magic awaits in each swirling mist.

Celestial Beasts Amongst the Shadows

When darkness falls and stars ignite,
The night unveils its wondrous sight.
Celestial beasts, with grace they roam,
Finding solace far from home.

With eyes like flames, they pierce the night,
As whispers echo in hushed delight.
Their paws tread softly on the skin of time,
Crafting a symphony so sublime.

In shadows deep, they weave and play,
Guardians of dreams that fade away.
Each roar a promise, each sigh a song,
In the heart of night where they belong.

Amongst the stars, their spirits soar,
Illuminating worlds never seen before.
Celestial wonders, fierce yet wise,
Under the watch of eternal skies.

So let your imagination take flight,
In the company of beasts of the night.
For in the shadows, you'll find they dare,
To dance with the moon, as if in prayer.

Reflections in the Misty Plume

In the hush of the dawn's soft glow,
Whispers dance where shadows flow.
Mirrored secrets in waters deep,
Guarded tales the silence keep.

Ripples weave through the tangled reeds,
Carrying thoughts like scattered seeds.
Each droplet holds a world untold,
In the mist, a magic bold.

The trees lean close, their branches bend,
Listening to the tales they send.
A symphony of sighs and dreams,
Caught within the twilight beams.

Glimmers spark as spirits play,
Beneath the clouds that drift away.
In fleeting moments, time stands still,
Shaping wonders with gentle will.

As sunbeams break the foggy chains,
Color bursts where hope remains.
A realm of shadows, light shall chase,
Unlocking secrets in this space.

Voices Hidden in the Fluffy Veil

In the depths of a twilight shroud,
Voices rise, both soft and loud.
Echoes linger in the air,
Hints of laughter, shades of care.

Clouds cascade like a wisping gown,
Draping softly over the town.
Within each fold, a story sings,
Hidden truths on fluttering wings.

A lantern flickers, shadows dance,
Illuminating fleeting chance.
In this veil, the heart may roam,
Seeking warmth to call it home.

Winds of tales begin to stir,
Fables whispered, soft as fur.
A tapestry of dreams entwined,
In every breath, a wish aligned.

Beneath the moon's enchanted glow,
Hidden voices start to flow.
In the quiet, magic thrives,
A world where every heartbeat lives.

Intricate Patterns of the Nebulous Coat

In the night where stars unfurl,
Patterns weave in a cosmic swirl.
Nebulas in colors bright,
Crafting tales of ancient flight.

Through the vastness, stories bloom,
Filling the dark, dispelling gloom.
A canvas rich with dreams relayed,
In every twist, life displayed.

Comets streak with fiery grace,
Leaving trails in the endless space.
Galaxies hum a lullaby,
Singing secrets to the sky.

Stardust falls like gentle rain,
Whispering hopes that wash away pain.
In the silence, wonders gleam,
In every heart, a sparkling dream.

With each pulse, the cosmos sighs,
As time and fate begin to rise.
In this coat of shades and light,
We find our truths in starry night.

Starlit Secrets of the Griffin's Hide

In the folds of an ancient skin,
Whispers of starlight dance within.
Griffin's gaze, fierce and wise,
Holds the cosmos in its eyes.

Feathers glimmer, tales unfold,
Stories lost, yet never old.
With each breath, the magic stirs,
Echoing the realm of furs.

Secrets linger in the air,
Twinkles shimmer, light to share.
In the depths of twilight gold,
Legends of the brave and bold.

The skies ignite with fiery dreams,
As the world below, in wonder, teems.
A guardian of tales untold,
With every leap, a myth unfolds.

Beneath the stars, a heart takes flight,
Chasing shadows, embracing light.
In the realms where fantasies abide,
We find the griffin as our guide.

Mysteries Worn in Nature's Garb

In shadows deep where secrets dwell,
The trees, they whisper, tales to tell.
With roots that twist like ancient fate,
Their bark conceals what time can't sate.

Among the leaves, a shimmer bright,
A fleeting glimpse of purest light.
The wild things dance, both fierce and free,
In harmony with mystery.

Each breeze that stirs, a hushed refrain,
Carries the echoes of lost pain.
The moon, a watchful guardian bold,
Unveils the stories yet untold.

Like threads of gold that stitch the seams,
Nature weaves in dreamy dreams.
Her colors speak in silent tones,
Amongst the roots, amidst the stones.

The flowers bloom in twilight's grace,
In every petal, a hidden place.
With secrets wrapped in softest green,
The heart of Earth remains unseen.

Lush Mists and Celestial Beasts

In morning's breath, the mists arise,
A veil that cloaks the waking skies.
With tender hues of silver gray,
The world transforms at break of day.

Within the shroud, a whisper glows,
Of wondrous things that nature knows.
From every shadow, wonders leap,
Where secrets in the silence creep.

Celestial beasts with wings of light,
Soar through the dreams of endless night.
With grace unmatched in winged flight,
They dance on breezes soft and slight.

A flicker here, a glinting spark,
Their laughter echoes through the dark.
They weave their paths 'midst fragrant blooms,
Crafting magic that brightly looms.

The lush mists weave their spell around,
In every breath, enchantment found.
Through every leaf and every stream,
The world awakens, bright as dream.

The Silken Shroud of Forgotten Lore

In twilight hours when shadows play,
The silken shroud drapes night and day.
With threads of silver, spun with care,
It holds the stories nestled there.

Whispers of ages long since passed,
In every fold, echoing fast.
The forgotten ones, they softly sigh,
Beneath the fabric of the sky.

A tapestry of dreams long gone,
Where time and memory both move on.
Their laughter lingers in the air,
A haunting tune, both sweet and rare.

Each stitch a spark of life once known,
Imprinted here on time's own throne.
The tales entwined in twilight's sweep,
Awaken visions from their sleep.

We seek the wisdom wrapped in night,
With longing hearts and spirits light.
To walk the paths of those before,
Entwined forever, lore to explore.

Gossamer Wings Beneath the Fog

In silent dawn, the fog descends,
A soft embrace where day transcends.
With gossamer wings, the fairies glide,
Through veils of mist, they sweetly hide.

The world blurs soft in vapor's kiss,
As nature breathes in blissful mist.
A tapestry of shades and hues,
Where secrets swirl like morning dews.

Among the shadows, laughter twirls,
As fairy lights form tiny swirls.
Each fluttered wing, a whispered word,
In fog's embrace, their magic stirred.

They weave their dreams in dusky folds,
With shimmering threads of fairy golds.
Through every nook, creations bloom,
In enchanting light amidst the gloom.

Beneath the fog, the stories blend,
Where spirits dance and hearts ascend.
In every breath, a wish takes flight,
With gossamer hopes, we greet the light.

Flickers of Life in Shrouded Woods

In the woods where shadows play,
Whispers dance on leaves so gray,
Flickers of life weave through the trees,
A tapestry made with gentle ease.

Sunlight filters, a golden beam,
Waking creatures from their dream,
Each rustle tells a tale anew,
Of magic hidden from our view.

Mossy paths where secrets creep,
Ancient roots in silence keep,
A flickering heart, a pulse so slight,
Guiding wanderers through the night.

Moonlit glades, a sacred space,
Where time slows its restless race,
In the shrouded woods, we find our way,
Lost in wonder, we dare to stay.

With every step, the magic grows,
In the soft earth where the wildflower blows,
Flickers of life, a brilliant spark,
Guide us home through the gathering dark.

Silhouettes Hidden in the Haze

Silhouettes dance in the evening mist,
With graceful forms, they twist and tryst,
Veiled in mystery, spun from dreams,
Echoes of laughter, soft silver streams.

Beneath the arches of ancient trees,
Whispers ride the drifting breeze,
Faint shadows play on paths unknown,
Each footfall soft, yet boldly sewn.

Haze wraps round as twilight glows,
In secret corners, enchantment flows,
Hidden wonders await the brave,
In the depths where the dauntless rave.

A flash of light, a fleeting glance,
In this realm, shadows dance,
Caught between the world and night,
Silhouettes hide from the fading light.

Yet still they linger, silent and strong,
In the haze where shadows throng,
Guiding us softly through the dark,
Illuminating paths with a flicker, a spark.

The Song of Timeless Guardians

In the heart of the ancient grove,
Where secrets flourish and ever rove,
Guardians stand with watchful eyes,
Singing softly beneath the skies.

Their voices knit a silken thread,
Binding past and future, gently spread,
Echoes of tales from ages long gone,
In every note, a history drawn.

With every lullaby, their strength remains,
In the rustling leaves, in the falling rains,
Timeless guardians, steadfast they sing,
Offering hope, a nurturing wing.

Through the shadows where dreams take flight,
They weave the fabric of day and night,
Every whisper a promise kept,
In this sanctuary where spirits wept.

So listen close, and you may find,
The song of guardians, pure and kind,
In the depths where wisdom thrives,
Lies the heart of all that survives.

Dreams Spun in Soft Enchantment

In twilight hours, where dreams take shape,
Magic weaves through the gentle drape,
Soft enchantment cloaks the mind,
In whispers of wonders, we seek and find.

Under the stars, with wishes bright,
We cast our hopes into the night,
Each breath a promise, a journey begun,
With dreams spun softly, one by one.

In the realm where fairies tread,
Where ancient stories softly spread,
Woven with care, the fabric's thread,
The enchantment blooms where heart is led.

Through the valleys of our desire,
We dance on air, our spirits higher,
Every shadow, a flicker of light,
Painting the canvas of the night.

With each dawn, the dreams take flight,
Guided by hope, resilient and bright,
In soft enchantment, we find our grace,
Eternal echoes in time and space.

Echoes in the Fogbound Fur

In the mist where whispers play,
Fur coats shimmer, light and gray.
Echoes of tales both dark and bright,
Hide in shadows, then take flight.

Paws tread softly on dampened ground,
Secrets in the silence found.
The world spins slowly, wrapped in hush,
As twilight beckons with a gentle crush.

Soft fur brushes the chill of night,
While distant calls weave through the light.
Each heartbeat dances with the fog,
Longing stirred by the night's warm bog.

Mystery swirls like the wispy breeze,
Veiling stories beneath the trees.
In this quiet, soft and stark,
Lives an echo with a spark.

As dawn unfolds her golden hue,
Fur shines bright, kissed by dew.
Yet in the stillness, shadows linger,
Echoes fading, their tales grow bigger.

Shadows Danced on Feathered Tapestry

In corners where the shadows play,
Feathered whispers twirl and sway.
A tapestry woven from night's soft breath,
Concealing secrets of life and death.

Moonlight drips like silken thread,
Embroidered dreams of those who fled.
Through darkened halls, the shadows weave,
Stories gathered, yet to leave.

Velvet wings brush against the light,
Carving paths through the velvet night.
Feathers drift like memories lost,
Seeking warmth, whatever the cost.

As dusk ignites the energy's surge,
From shadows, strange visions emerge.
In flickers of dance and soft refrain,
Starlight glimmers, alive with pain.

Yet morning laughs, and shadows flee,
Leaving traces for eyes to see.
On feathered tapestries so grand,
The dance continues, a guiding hand.

Whispers of the Twilight Threads

In twilight's grasp, the threads do hum,
Whispers soft as the night's sweet drum.
Silk and shadow in soft embrace,
Weave a world, a hidden place.

Fingers trace the patterns spun,
Across horizons where day is done.
The threads vibrate with secrets told,
In hues of lavender and gold.

Styles shift as the night persists,
Through tangled strands, the silence twists.
Moonlit fabric, a canvas bright,
Threads of day fading into night.

In the stillness, the magic flows,
Each whispered thread in twilight glows.
Dancing softly, the stories wait,
A tapestry woven with fate.

As dawn approaches with gentle sighs,
The whispers fade as the shadows rise.
Yet through the day, their echoes cling,
In the heart of the threads, life will sing.

Enigmas of the Clouded Pelage

In the mist of mystery's embrace,
Clouded pelage hides a face.
Each flicker of fur tells a tale,
Hints of magic in every trail.

Mysteries linger like morning dew,
Wrapped in secrets, the world anew.
Patterns twist in the lingering night,
Tethered paths that fade from sight.

Whispers low in the verdant thicket,
Soft and dark, where shadows thicket.
Hidden wonders beneath the skin,
In the clouded fur, tales begin.

Like riddles sung by a gentle breeze,
The heart discovers, searching with ease.
Soft pelage wraps the unknown,
Burdened yet tender, forever grown.

As the sun weaves through foliage tight,
The enigmas dance, banishing fright.
In the journey of fur and mist,
Life pulses forth, magic in every twist.

The Hushed Beauty of Clouded Mane

In the meadow where shadows play,
The whispers of twilight softly sway.
A dance of silver, subtle and fine,
Clouded manes shimmer, a secret sign.

Beneath the gaze of the waning light,
Silhouettes meld into the night.
Each breath of wind tells tales anew,
Of ancient pasts wrapped in dew.

With a pulse of magic, they roam so free,
In the realm where none can see.
Their beauty hidden, yet ever present,
A mystical bond—a gift, a crescent.

Glimmers of hope in dusk's embrace,
With every step, the soft earth's grace.
They scatter dreams on star-strewn ground,
Where whispered wonders will ever abound.

So cherish the hush as shadows fade,
In the twilight dance of the serenade.
For beauty cloaked in twilight's veil,
Is a fleeting wish on a silvery trail.

Tints of Enigma in the Fluffed Realm

In a world where colors softly blend,
Fluffed realms whisper, secrets to send.
Each hue a note in a song untold,
Draped in mysteries, both bright and bold.

Soft pastels curl like tendrils of air,
A hint of laughter lingers, so rare.
Here, every shade tells a story unclear,
A palette of dreams, both far and near.

Shadows pirouette in a swirling dance,
In this realm of enigma, take a chance.
The tints of twilight merge into one,
As the sky greets the advent of sun.

Fluttering whispers intertwine in flight,
Wings brush the canvas painted by night.
In soft glow, the unknown awaits,
To unfurl its gifts, as fate contemplates.

So dwell in the hues of a waking dream,
Where nothing is ever quite as it seems.
In every glance, a riddle or clue,
A magic that's waiting, just for you.

Elegies of the Faintly Feathered

Beneath the sky in muted grace,
Faintly feathered, a slow embrace.
Whispers carried on gentle wings,
In the softest hymn, remembrance sings.

The echo of flight through dreamy air,
Every heartbeat a silent prayer.
In shadows flickering, they glide and weave,
Spirits of twilight, destined to leave.

A tapestry woven of hopes and fears,
Carried aloft through the quiet years.
In each soft flutter, a tale is spun,
Elegies caught in the setting sun.

When dusk holds the world in its tender hand,
The faintly feathered understand.
For every ending, there lies a start,
In whispers of wind, they touch the heart.

So mourn their flight with compassion's grace,
As memories linger in time's embrace.
For every feather that slips away,
A new dawn beckons—a bright array.

Fables of the Cumulus Coat

In skies where dreams and clouds entwine,
Cumulus coats weave stories divine.
Each layer whispers, drifting on high,
Fables of time woven in the sky.

Bulbous and soft as a child's delight,
They cradle the whispers of endless flight.
Every puffy shape a thought in bloom,
A canvas of wonder, dispelling gloom.

Gentle giants who roam astray,
In the playful dance of the light of day.
Each puff a promise, a tale unfurled,
In the beholder's eye—a new world.

So let your mind soar amidst the white,
Through fluffy realms and realms of light.
For in the skies where these fables are spun,
Innocence lingers, and dreams have begun.

So breathe in the magic, let freedom reign,
As the spirit of clouds calls you again.
Cumulus coats in a playful roam,
The sky is a story—imagination's home.

Treading the Misted Pathways

Beneath the silvered moonlight's glow,
A path of whispers beckons slow,
Through veils of mist, where shadows play,
And dreams of night invite the day.

The trees stand tall, a sentinel,
Enchanted tales they have to tell,
With each soft step, the world unfolds,
Revealing secrets, brave and bold.

In twilight's breath, the stars will spark,
To light the way through realms of dark,
The air is thick with magic's art,
As hearts unite, a shared sweet start.

From every corner, echoes sigh,
Of laughter lost, or softly cry,
A journey forged on misty ground,
Where memories linger, love is found.

So tread the pathways, rare and bright,
Embrace the shadows, seek the light,
For here in magic, life will sway,
In treading paths of yesterday.

A Lullaby of Intangible Beasts

In moonlit glades where shadows creep,
The creatures dwell, their secrets keep,
With glimmering eyes and whispered grace,
They dance beyond our waking space.

Furry phantoms, soft and fleet,
With velvet paws and hearts so sweet,
They roam the realms we cannot see,
In twilight dreams, they wander free.

A tune of stars in gentle flight,
They sing to us beneath the night,
A lullaby of dreams untold,
In softest warmth, our hearts they hold.

With every flutter, every sigh,
They weave a spell, a lullaby,
And in their song, the world dissolves,
In mysteries where love evolves.

So let your mind in slumber drift,
To where the unseen spirits lift,
In twilight's embrace, let dreams find rest,
A lullaby of beasts, the very best.

Celestial Drizzles and Plush Secrets

The stars descend in gentle drops,
Caressing earth, where silence stops,
With whispers soft, celestial tunes,
And dreams unfold beneath the moons.

In silver drizzles, wishes bloom,
While night unveils its velvet gloom,
Plush secrets float on midnight wings,
As starlight dances, softly sings.

Each glimmer holds a tale to share,
Of wandering souls and hearts laid bare,
In every droplet, magic gleams,
Awakening our wondrous dreams.

So gather 'round, embrace the night,
Where every shadow, every light,
Bears stories wrapped in soft-spun grace,
In celestial drizzles, find your place.

For while the heavens softly weep,
They bless our hearts, our souls to keep,
In the plush warmth of nature's sigh,
Where dreams of stars shall never die.

The Dance of Silhouettes in Twilight

In twilight's hush, silhouettes sway,
As dusk unfurls its soft array,
They move with grace, both wild and free,
A dance of shadows, you and me.

The world is cloaked in dusky dreams,
Where nothing's ever what it seems,
With laughter laced in whispers low,
And secrets wrapped in evening's glow.

The air is thick with stories bold,
Of adventures waiting to be told,
In every flicker, a spark ignites,
As shadows merge with gentle lights.

Each step a heartbeat, echoing sweet,
In rhythm with the night's heartbeat,
They twirl through moments, crafting fate,
A timeless dance, where dreams await.

So let the silhouettes embrace,
The mystery and the whispered grace,
For in this twilight, love will find,
A dance of souls, forever entwined.

Embrace of the Elusive Echo

In the forest deep, where shadows creep,
An echo dances, soft and sweet.
Through whispering leaves, it gently glows,
A tale of ages, no one knows.

Beneath the moon's pale, silver beam,
The night unveils a timeless dream.
With every step, the heartbeat sings,
Awakening magic that twilight brings.

Footfalls silent, yet hearts aflame,
In the embrace of an ancient name.
A call to wander, a path unclear,
Yet filled with wonders, boundless, dear.

Hope entwined with every sigh,
A fleeting glimpse of the sky-high.
In the echo's arms, lost souls find,
A fleeting bond of heart and mind.

So heed the call, and drift away,
Embrace the night, let shadows play.
For in this magic, joy shall swell,
Through the embrace of the elusive spell.

Threads of Mystery in the Twilight

As twilight drapes the world in blue,
Threads of mystery weave anew.
In every corner, secrets sigh,
Beneath the watchful, twinkling sky.

The breeze carries stories from afar,
Of distant lands and a shining star.
Each whispered tale, a tapestry spun,
In the twilight glow, our hearts are one.

Beneath the arch of the dusky night,
Every shadow dances with pure delight.
With every moment, the silence grows,
A canvas unfolding, where wonder flows.

In the hush of dusk, new worlds emerge,
The heartbeats quicken; dreams converge.
With fingers intertwined in fate,
We journey forth, it's never too late.

So weave the threads with care and grace,
In twilight's embrace, find your place.
For in the whispers of the night,
Lies the promise of magic's light.

Whispers from the Celestial Grove

In the celestial grove, where stardust glows,
Whispers of secrets the gentle wind knows.
Through branches laden with moonlit sighs,
The heart bears witness to the night's soft cries.

Every rustle tells of dreams yet seen,
Of worlds beyond, where souls convene.
In the shimmer of leaves, the voles retreat,
Where shadows linger, forever discreet.

Beneath the gaze of the silver sphere,
Each tender breath rings crystal clear.
In this sacred space of night's embrace,
Hope whispers softly, love leaves its trace.

With every heartbeat, the cosmos spins,
And dreams take flight on celestial winds.
Among the echoes of time and space,
The grove unfolds its warm embrace.

So linger a while in twilight's tune,
As stars awaken and the night is strewn.
For whispers here will guide your heart,
In the celestial grove, where wonders start.

Glistening Feathers in the Fog

In the shrouded mist, where secrets lie,
Glistening feathers flutter and fly.
Each drop of dew, a dream retold,
Of adventures waiting, bright and bold.

The fog entwines with shadows of grace,
Embracing lost souls in its silent space.
With every breath, the magic grows,
In the dance of the night, where the wild wind blows.

Beneath the cloak of the velvet night,
Feathers shimmer, reflecting light.
In every flutter, a promise glows,
As the heart awakens and softly knows.

So walk the path where the whispers dwell,
In the stillness, hear the stories tell.
For in fog's embrace and feathered song,
We find the echoes to which we belong.

Glistening wonders, a sight to see,
In the fog's gentle arms, we are free.
So follow the light where the feathers guide,
In the mystery of night, let joy abide.

Wisps of Enchantment in the Mist

In the glade where shadows play,
Whispers weave through twilight's sway.
Moonlit beams on water's crest,
Breath of magic, softly blessed.

Gossamer threads in the air,
Dancing dreams, beyond compare.
Each dew drop, a story spun,
Of ancient spells and races run.

Beneath the cloak of misty grey,
Mystics gather, come what may.
They chant the tales of yore,
Unlocking secrets from the lore.

Faintest echoes, laughter's sound,
Round the corners of the ground.
Heartbeats match the night's embrace,
In the ever-twisting space.

So let your soul take to the night,
Embrace the shadows, seek the light.
For in this realm of pure delight,
Wisps of enchantment take their flight.

Fables Woven in the Wind

On the breeze where stories blend,
Whispers of the past, they send.
Through the trees, a tale takes flight,
Fables carried through the night.

Every leaf a page unturned,
In the heart where passion burned.
Murmurs soft like ancient songs,
Tell of righting all the wrongs.

Clouds like pages, drifting free,
Painted themes of destiny.
Histories in gales unfurled,
Magic spun across the world.

Twilight dances, dreams arise,
In the fabric of the skies.
Threads of laughter, tears, and pain,
Woven tightly, never plain.

So listen closely, hear the tune,
From the earth beneath the moon.
For in the wind, a tale you'll find,
Fables whispered, intertwined.

The Ethereal Dance of Guardian Spirits

In the twilight's gentle breath,
Spirits stir, eluding death.
Draped in light, they twirl and sway,
Guiding souls who lost their way.

By the brook where secrets sigh,
Guardian forms with watchful eye.
Every flicker, every glance,
Invites the heart to dare and dance.

With shimmering wings like stars,
They weave through night, erasing scars.
Hands entwined, they paint the sky,
With wishes whispered, never shy.

Through the forest, shadows weave,
Guardians teach, to dream, believe.
In their arms, the world feels whole,
Cradled deep within the soul.

So close your eyes, and feel the flow,
Of spirits guiding where to go.
In this ethereal, soft embrace,
You'll find your heart's most sacred place.

Shadows Beneath a Mystical Canopy

Beneath the bows of ancient trees,
Whispers carried by the breeze.
Lights and shadows blend and play,
In a world that slips away.

Fern and moss, a carpet deep,
Where the dreams of ancients sleep.
Echoes of a time long past,
In the twilight, shadows cast.

Listen close, the secrets dwell,
In the stories nature tells.
Every rustle, every sigh,
Holds a truth that will not die.

As the sun dips, colors fade,
Night descends, a velvet shade.
Stars peek through the leafy veil,
In this land, enchantments hail.

So wander long, where magic calls,
Feel the comfort of these halls.
For beneath this mystical sky,
Shadows dance, and spirits fly.

Envelopes of Dreamlike Wool

In shadows spun from twilight's grace,
Dreams are wrapped in soft embrace.
With whispers woven, tender, light,
They dance beneath the silver night.

Soft tendrils of a fleeting thought,
In cozy corners, silence caught.
The mind unravels, fears take flight,
As starlit wishes spark the night.

Through realms where slumber often calls,
In gentle hushed and velvet halls.
Each heartbeat echoes, sweet and low,
Through knitted paths where dreamers go.

With threads of hope in colors bright,
The fabric of the heart takes flight.
Each secret sigh, each tearful swell,
Is wrapped in magic only time can tell.

So hold your dreams, let whispers flow,
In this embrace of endless glow.
For in each stitch and woven thread,
Lies life's true tale, both unspoken and said.

Whirlwinds of Misty Textures

In swirling shapes where shadows play,
The whispers of the wind will sway.
Through textures fine, and colors blend,
A tale of wonder without end.

The misty dance, a soft caress,
In secret echoes, feel the press.
Each gust reveals what lies beneath,
The hidden paths of dreams we sheath.

As swirling tales in breezes twirl,
A symphony of softest whirl.
The earth and sky in rhythms meet,
As whispers rise beneath our feet.

With every breath, the world exhales,
In fleeting turns, where mystery trails.
And in each gust, a story spins,
Of hidden truths and softly wins.

So let the currents wrap you tight,
In textures of the fading light.
For in the whirlwinds' gentle scheme,
We find the fabric of our dream.

Beneath the Veil of Feathered Mists

Beneath a veil of whispers soft,
The feathered mists, they rise aloft.
In twilight shades, where secrets hide,
Imagination flows like tide.

The world in hues of muted grace,
Creates a peace, a sacred space.
With every breath, the air is sweet,
As visions gather at our feet.

In gentle folds, the shadows stir,
While echoes whisper, faint, demur.
With every heartbeat, love entwined,
In mists that veil the dreamers' mind.

As night descends with silent plea,
Through veils of fog, we long to see.
What lies beyond, a soft embrace,
In memory's tender, timeless space.

So let us wander, hearts set free,
In twilight's dance where we shall be,
Drawn deep beneath the mists unfurled,
To find our place within the world.

Secrets in the Gossamer Shadows

In shadows woven, secrets sigh,
Like whispers felt but never nigh.
Gossamer threads, both fine and spun,
Tell tales of moonlight's quiet fun.

Each twinkling star, a hidden clue,
In twilight's grasp, a tale anew.
The secrets linger, soft and sweet,
In every fold and silent beat.

The night reveals its gentle art,
Where every line plays lover's part.
In shadows cast by flickering flame,
We find the world will never tame.

With every flick and gentle sway,
We seek the truth in shadows gray.
For hidden there in twilight glow,
Are mysteries only dreamers know.

So let us dance on silken light,
In gossamer shadows, take our flight.
For in the night where secrets lie,
Our hearts will soar, our spirits fly.

Epiphanies in the Faded Whorl

In twilight's glow, secrets dance,
Whispers weave through shadows' chance.
Old stones stir with tales untold,
Dreams awaken, glimmers bold.

A flicker glows in a rusted key,
Unlocking doors no one can see.
Time bends softly, a gentle sigh,
Epiphanies bloom, as moments fly.

In gardens where the wild things play,
Forgotten hearts now find their way.
Each petal's drop, a tale thus spun,
A tapestry where worlds are one.

In the stillness, echoes reign,
Memories dance, a sweet refrain.
Every breath holds magic near,
In faded whorls, we persevere.

The Shroud of Enchantment and Wonder

Beneath the arch of starlit skies,
Where shadows whisper and magic lies,
A shroud of dreams, so soft, so deep,
Cradles hearts that yearn to leap.

In twilight's embrace, hope stirs awake,
A symphony of wishes, a bond we make.
With every flicker, a promise unfolds,
Enchantment blooms, mysteries hold.

Tales spin forth from the silken thread,
While faeries dance where the brave dare tread.
In moonlit glades, the world transforms,
Awakening wonders, as magic warms.

The night is rich with secrets spun,
Revealing paths where dreams have run.
In every breath, the wondrous flow,
A shroud of tales that softly glow.

Tales Lurking in the Soft Haze

In a realm where the mist entwines,
Lurking tales weave through the pines.
Soft haze blankets the waking ground,
In silence, the stories abound.

With every step, whispers confide,
The trees hold secrets, the scene alive.
Ghostly echoes from ages past,
In shadows linger, memories cast.

Around the bend, laughter flickers bright,
Ghostly figures weave through the night.
In soft embrace, the world retells,
Tales of enchantment where wonder dwells.

The moon hangs low, a guiding light,
Illuminating dreams that take flight.
In every shadow, curiosities blaze,
For magic thrives in the soft haze.

Unraveling Mysteries of the Fluffy Embrace

In a world of clouds, soft and wide,
Mysteries linger a gentle tide.
Fluffy embrace cradles the soul,
Where dreams ignite and secrets roll.

Beneath the fluff adventures lie,
Waiting for hearts brave enough to try.
Wistful journeys on cotton trails,
A tapestry woven whispered tales.

On the journey, laughter will bloom,
As the fluffy embrace dispels all gloom.
With arms of warmth captures the heart,
In its cradle, we'll never part.

As dawn breaks softly, colors unfurl,
Promises dance in wondrous swirl.
Unraveled by hope, we take our place,
In the embrace of this fluffy grace.

9 781805 645429